ONCE UPON A TIME IN RHYME

28 Folk and Fairy Tale Poems and Songs

by Meish Goldish

SCHOLASTIC
PROFESSIONAL BOOKS

NEW YORK • TORONTO • LONDON • AUCKLAND • SYDNEY

Cover design by Vincent Ceci and Frank Maiocco
Interior design by Jacqueline Swensen
Cover and interior illustration by Jan Pyk
Front matter and activities by Mary Beth Spann

ISBN 0-590-48801-5

TABLE OF CONTENTS

MULTICULTURAL TALES

AMERICAN FOLKLORE

INTRODUCTION

Welcome to *Once Upon a Time in Rhyme*! Here, the classic stories children love have been reworked as rousing, rhyming poems and songs for you and your students to enjoy whenever you wish. Childhood singing and chanting is a part of cultures around the world, so this collection fits right in with what comes naturally to students everywhere. Like other favorite poems and songs, those in this book are easy to listen to and a joy to perform. Their language is playful and alive with rhythm and rhyme. Each toe-tapping selection begs children to join in and be part of the storytelling fun: singing, swaying, wiggling, waving, acting out, moving, doing and creating.

In addition to providing you with 28 ready-to-use fables and fairy tales, this book offers creative "Suggestions for Sharing" each selection, including ideas for fostering students' participation. It also contains "Extension Activities" designed to link each selection to other areas of the curriculum.

The best part of the collection is that you can truly make it your own. Feel free to mix and match the suggestions for sharing. Dream up your own extension activities. Invite students' participation by encouraging them to sing, retell, or illustrate the selections. Use this book as a springboard for exploring the rich world of fable and fairy tales together!

HOW TO USE THIS BOOK

This book contains 28 folk and fairy tales, each presented as a chant or as a song set to a familiar tune. Here are some before and after suggestions for sharing each one with your students.

Before Sharing Aloud

TURN POEMS AND SONGS INTO CHARTS

Before attempting to share the selections in class, it is recommended that you print each one clearly on a large piece of chart pad paper or oaktag. Consider laminating your charts. Then, after students use markers to illustrate and write on the charts, you can just wipe the charts clean with a damp sponge or a baby wipe.

The teacher resource book *Building Literacy with Interactive Charts: A Practical Guide for Creating 75 Engaging Charts from Songs, Poems and Fingerplays* by Kristin G. Schlosser and Vicki L. Phillips (Scholastic, 1992) has lots of ideas and resources you'll find helpful when charting the fairy tales and fables in this book.

PUT CHARTS ON DISPLAY

Display your charts on a chart holder or easel set up in one special spot in your classroom. Or, integrate the charts into your already-established Poetry Corner. When you've completed your work with any one song or poem chart, move them into the hallway for other classes to enjoy.

PLAN AHEAD

Before sharing selections in class, give a bit of thought to the possible reasons you want children to experience each one:

- Do you just want to share it once or twice for fun with no follow-up needed?
- Will a selection complement an existing theme unit you already teach?
- Do you plan to use a particular selection to help students learn a language or writing skill (such as identifying rhyming words)?
- Will students perform the selection for an audience or simply act it out as you perform it for them?
- Or, perhaps you wish to simply share and discuss a selection as a pure listening activity before showing the printed selection on the chart.

In any case, it's certainly not necessary or desirable to expect children to be able to read or memorize all the words to any one chant or song. Better to expect they will participate by identifying or learning some of the words or lines (such as the chorus parts) to some of the selections. (Tip: Sometimes its best to see how a selection strikes a group of children before deciding how important it will become in your curriculum.)

COLLECT RELATED RESOURCES

When planning to share a selection, consider collecting other versions of the same fable or fairy tale to offer to your class at the same time. In this way, students can be exposed to different treatments of the same story. This offers students an opportunity to learn to respect different perspectives and to realize there is no one right way to tell a tale.

Also, consider assembling some adult resources for yourself and parents, such as *Crackers and Crumbs: Chants for Whole Language* by Sonja Dunn with Lou Pamenter (Pembroke Publishers, 1990).

ASSEMBLE PROPS, COSTUMES AND MUSICAL INSTRUMENTS

You can certainly share any of the selections in this book without using one prop, costume or instrument—but using them certainly enriches the experience! Specific suggestions for using such enhancements accompany each of the selections, and, of course, you and your students will have wonderful ideas of your own.

Remember, it's best to keep things simple. As you work your way through the book, jot a list of easy-to-obtain props and costume ideas children can use when acting out each selection. (You might enlist a parent's help here—even a working parent can take on the task of collecting the items on your lists.) Or, suggest that children scour their homes and the classroom to come up with such creative dramatic supplies. Store items gathered in a creative drama "trunk," which can consist of a large cardboard carton spray-painted with metallic paint or a discarded toy box salvaged from a rummage or yard sale.

Consider borrowing rhythm instruments from early childhood teachers and ask children to bring in instruments from home. Also consider using handcrafted instruments you create in class such as rice-filled plastic containers or pie tin "drums" with pencil drumsticks. Again, encourage the children's suggestions for making beautiful noises to accompany the poems and songs. Keep in mind that feet and hands are always at the ready for clapping and stomping out any song or chant you wish.

PREVIEW THE SELECTIONS

Before sharing selections in class, read or sing each selection aloud to yourself. When you have experienced each selection's rhythm and cadence firsthand, you can better pass it on to your students.

Suggestions for Presenting Poems and Songs in Class

ESTABLISH PRIOR KNOWLEDGE

Introduce a new poem or song by asking children to tell how many are familiar with the folk, fable, or fairy tale at hand. Ask students familiar with the tale to recap the story or to recall any details they can remember. Tell students you will be sharing a different version of the story they know. Ask them to listen to how the poem or the song may be the same as or different from the version they know. The first time through, consider chanting or singing the selection for your class without having the children refer to the lyrics on the chart. If children are not familiar with any one story, offer a brief summary culled from the background information that follows each one in the book.

INTRODUCE THE SONG OR CHANT TO THE CLASS

When presenting a song or chant to the class, it can be desirable to have students just listen for the first few sharings before including the selection on a chart. Begin by singing or reading the chant through, then ask for the children's responses to the selection (what the selection was about, their most or least favorite part, etc.) Immediately follow this first sharing with a second. This time, clap or use a rhythm instrument to keep the beat. Ask children to join in as they wish (keeping time or repeating the chorus). Now you are ready to show the class the selection on the chart.

SHARE THE CHARTED SONG OR CHANT

Prominently display the chant or song chart so all can see. Carefully read the lyrics through, underscoring each line with a pointer or with your hand, if you wish. Then, perform the selection at a lively pace. Encourage students to join in performing the chant or the song when and where they wish. (Tip: If you wish students to learn a particular selection or part of a selection, try having children be your "echoes"—repeating each designated line after you sing or recite it. Students should also be encouraged to take turns using the pointer with the charts.)

USE SENTENCE STRIPS

As an option to printing the poems or songs on chart paper, consider using sentence strips to record each line of a selection. When finally ready to share the selection, you can offer children lines to hold and listen for. Then, as you sing or read the selection aloud, children can place their lines in sequence in the pockets of a sentence strip holder or glue their strips in correct order to a piece of chart pad paper.

TRY STICKY NOTE LESSONS

During subsequent sessions, you may want students to listen to the selection then look at the corresponding chart to locate particular letters, parts of speech, sound patterns, rhyming words, etc. A supply of different-sized removable sticky notes can prove invaluable. Children can use these notes to:

❀ flag words beginning with the same letter (or those containing the same vowel sound, etc.);

❀ identify rhyming words;

❀ highlight nouns, verbs, adjectives, etc;

❀ cover words for classmates to guess;

❀ identify different characters' dialogue;

❀ separate stanzas so different groups in the class will know which part they are to sing or recite;

❀ write substitutions for lyrics;

❀ draw illustrations for temporarily covering up words, thus turning the chart into a rebus story.

MAKE STUDENT COPIES AVAILABLE

Try providing individual copies of each selection to students who may then use crayons or markers to:

❀ underline portions of the selection they are responsible for performing individually or as part of a small group;

❀ highlight each character's dialogue (have students use a separate color for each one);

❀ add illustrations to the selections;

❀ circle any words they cannot read or do not understand (or any favorite words, or any particular parts of speech, etc.);

❀ circle rhyming word pairs;

❀ identify the same letter (or word or phrase) as it appears throughout the selection.

Cross-Curricular Follow-up Activities

If all you do with this collection of rhyming fables and fairy tales is perform them aloud, your students will be better for the experience. But, if you really want to enhance the learning, you'll try some of the related activities as described above and throughout the book. In addition, you'll want to experiment with some of the following ideas for linking the poems and songs to every area of the curriculum.

ASSEMBLE A FAIRY TALE AND FABLE ANTHOLOGY

Mount a copy of the lyrics to each song and chant on a construction paper "mat." Have each child work alone or with a partner to illustrate at least one selection. Punch three holes down the left-hand margin of each page. Use ribbon to bind the pages together between construction paper covers. Title the book "Fable and Fairy Tale Poems and Songs." Place the book in your library corner for children to enjoy. Make the anthology available to students to take home and share with family members.

CREATE A BULLETIN BOARD DISPLAY

Place a chart in the middle of a bulletin board. Decide together which parts of the selection students should illustrate. Then, offer students chart paper and art supplies (pencils, paints, markers, crayons and scissors) so they can draw and color the story elements you decided upon. Help students design their illustrations so they are not too small or too large for the display. Cut out the illustrations and post each one around the display. (Tip: Consider outlining each illustration with black marker so it stands out on the display. Also, when displaying characters who have lines of dialogue in the song or chant, try creating paper dialogue balloons complete with dialogue to place near each character's mouth.)

PREPARE SEQUENCE PUZZLES

Some of the poems and songs (such as "The Three Little Pigs") feature a storyline that unfolds in a linear sequence. Make copies of these and cut the verses apart. Place the pieces into an envelope. Students must then read the song or chant and glue the pieces in the correct order onto a whole piece of paper. (If necessary, students may refer to the chart or an uncut copy for puzzle clues.)

MAKE MULTIMEDIA CONNECTIONS

Many of the stories featured in this collection are available as video productions. Send home a list of the book's table of contents and ask families to read through the titles and to lend any related videos for classroom viewing. Also, check out your local library and video store for such video availability. Be sure to preview any selections you plan to show to make sure they are appropriate for your class. Just before viewing a video in class, share the song or chant it relates to. As you sing or recite, ask children to close their eyes and "see" a moving picture of the story in their minds. After viewing a show, ask students to tell how the show's pictures differed from those they had already created in their minds. As a follow-up, consider making a video film of students acting out their favorite stories. Send these films home, along with copies of the stories, for families to enjoy together.

PUT ON A FABLE AND FAIRY TALE PRODUCTION

With a bit of practice, you can easily use this collection of poems and songs as the basis for a school play production. First, ask for student input and together select several favorites to perform. Then, think up simple props and costumes for acting out each one. Select different students to perform each selection. (Student performers can be part of a crowd scene before and after the selection in which they will "star." The crowd can sing or recite the selection together as the stars pantomime the actions.) To boost the sound quality of your production (and to guard against students forgetting lyrics), try tape recording students singing or reciting each selection ahead of time (or use the prerecorded tape that is available with this book). Then, have the live performers sing or recite along with the tape.) As a background for your production, consider displaying the illustrated posters that accompany each selection.

THROW A CHARACTER BALL

As a wrap-up to your study of fables and fairy tales, hold a Character Ball where students come to school dressed as their favorite fable and fairy tale characters. For costume inspiration, have students browse through illustrated collections you've assembled. Plan to have appropriate refreshments on hand such as gingerbread boy cookies, pretzel logs (commemorating "Paul Bunyan"), pigs in a blanket (soy hot dogs cut into pieces, wrapped in quick popover dough and baked in a toaster oven for 15 minutes at 375° to accompany "The Three Little Pigs") and grapes and grape juice (inspired by "The Fox and the Grapes"). Be sure to label each snack so lots of meaningful reading can take place along with the munching!

For entertainment, have children play a guessing game whereby they each offer classmates clues to his or her identity. As each character's identity is revealed, pin an identifying label on each costume. Finish up by traveling to other classes to perform your favorite fable and fairy tale poems and songs.

ONCE UPON A TIME IN RHYME

28 Folk and Fairy Tale Poems and Songs

The Three Little Pigs

(sung to "My Grandfather's Clock")

The three little pigs had to each build a house
So they'd each keep the wolf from their door.
The first little pig built a thin house of straw
So that he would be free to play more.
When the wolf came along, piggy's house was not so strong.
"Let me in!" cried the wolf with a blast!
Then he huffed! Puffed! Blew the straw house down,
And the pig ran fast!

The next little pig had to put up a house
So that he'd keep the wolf from his door.
The next little pig built a thin house of twigs
So that he would be free to play more.
When the wolf came along, piggy's house was not so strong.
"Let me in!" cried the wolf with a blast!
Then he huffed! Puffed! Blew the twig house down,
And the pig ran fast!

The third little pig had to put up a house
So that he'd keep the wolf from his door.
The third little pig built a strong house of bricks,
Though it took time and work for the chore.
When the wolf came along, piggy's house was very strong.
"Let me in!" cried the wolf with a blast!
Then he huffed! Puffed! But couldn't blow it down,
For the bricks held fast!

There's a lesson to learn here, learn it, learn it!
To have something good, you must earn it, earn it!
So huff! Puff! Put in the time and work,
So your work will last!

TEACHER'S PAGE

ABOUT THE STORY

"The Three Little Pigs" is an old English fairy tale. In the original version, the first two pigs are eaten by the wolf. In the more modern telling, the lazy pigs are saved by the industrious pig, who offers them refuge in his house. But in all versions, the wolf ends up being boiled in a pot of water after attempting to climb down the brick chimney. The lesson of the story is clear: Hard work, though not always fun, pays off in the end.

SUGGESTIONS FOR SHARING

Cut three separate pieces of oaktag into three house shapes—one for each litttle pig. First, trim two corners of each piece so it resembles a roof. Then, after talking with children about the features they might find on a house facade (roof shingles, windows, door, etc.) provide children with art supplies (paints, brushes and markers) so they may decorate the houses to look like those belonging to the Three Little Pigs. As the song is sung, children can take turns holding the first two houses upright until the wolf (played by another child or a puppet) comes along and blows them down. The brick house can be attached with glue to a heavy piece of cardboard so that it cannot be blown down. (Tip: If your box is large enough, it may be used as a drama trunk for storing costumes or props related to this or any other song or poem in this book.)

EXTENSION ACTIVITY (MATH/ORGANIZATIONAL SKILLS)

Have children note architectural details featured on the interior and exterior of their school building and homes. Ask students to research what materials went into building these structures and, in particular, what materials help make the buildings strong. After looking closely at how bricks and cinder blocks are arranged in real buildings, have children experiment with cardboard bricks to see which stacking arrangements are strongest. Arrange for your school's maintenance personnel to give your class a tour of your school's structural underpinnings. In this way, children can see for themselves how much work and thought must go into designing and planning a permanent structure.

LITERATURE LINKS

The Three Little Pigs retold by Sally Bell, illustrated by J. Ellen Dolce. New York: Golden Books, 1991.

The Three Little Pigs retold by Marcia Leonard, illustrated by Doug Cushman. Englewood Cliffs, NJ: Silver Press, 1990.

The True Story of the 3 Little Pigs by A. Wolf, as told to Jon Scieszka, illustrated by Lane Smith. New York: Scholastic, 1991.

Goldilocks and the Three Bears

Goldilocks came to a house in the woods.
Inside all was quiet.
She saw cereal in three different bowls
And said, "I think I'll try it."

"The first bowl is much too hot.
The second's too cold—I hate it!
But the third bowl tastes just right!"
So Goldie quickly ate it!

Goldilocks went to another room.
Inside all was quiet.
She found three chairs, looked at each,
And said, "I think I'll try it."

"The first chair is much too hard.
The second's too soft, I fear.
But the third chair feels just right!"
Then she sat and broke it! Oh, dear!

Goldilocks next climbed into a bed,
And after she closed her eyes,
The three bears came back to their home
And found her—what a surprise!

"Who's in my bed?" cried Baby Bear.
"Who's that in our house?"
Goldilocks awoke and ran away
As quickly as a mouse.

TEACHER'S PAGE

ABOUT THE STORY

"Goldilocks and the Three Bears" is based on an old nursery tale made popular in 1837 by English poet Robert Southey. In the original version, the house intruder was a troublesome old woman. Over the years, however, the character changed to a young girl—first named Silverhair, and later, Goldilocks.

SUGGESTIONS FOR SHARING

Offer children a copy of the poem. Point out that any time quotation marks frame words, it means someone is speaking those words. Have children identify who is speaking in the poem (i.e., Goldilocks and Baby Bear). Have children use a yellow crayon to highlight Goldilock's monologue. Then, have them use a green crayon to highlight Baby Bear's monologue. Have children decide on distinctly different voices for the two characters, such as a high voice for Goldilocks and a growley bear voice for Baby Bear. Acting as narrator, read the poem through, pausing at the quotations so the class can read the dialogue lines in unison.

EXTENSION ACTIVITY (LANGUAGE ARTS/SEQUENCING SKILLS)

Share with children a variety of versions of the Three Bear's story. Then, have children make a list of dolls and props (i.e., doll furniture, dishes, doll house) they might need to retell the story. Have children bring in items on the list. Then have children work together to pose their dolls and props to represent various scenes in the story. Have children take photographs of each scene. When the pictures are developed, have children place the photos in sequential order into an album along with a written or dictated caption for each one. Fill in any necessary text so that, when read in order, the pictures and captions retell the story of Goldilocks and the Three Bears.

LITERATURE LINKS

Goldilocks by Dom DeLuise, illustrated by Christopher Santoro. New York: Simon & Schuster Books for Young Readers, 1992.

Goldilocks by Tom Roberts, illustrated by Laszlo Kubinyi. Westport, CT: Rabbit Ears Books, 1990.

Goldilocks and the Three Bears retold by Jonathan Langley. New York: HarperCollins, 1993.

The Gingerbread Man

(sung to "Jimmy Crack Corn")

A baker took some ginger dough
And shaped a man from head to toe.
When it was baked, the cookie fled.
Here is what the cookie said:

CHORUS:
Run! Run! As fast as you can!
You can't catch me, I'm the gingerbread man!
Run! Run! As fast as you can!
I'm the gingerbread man!

The cookie man ran past a cow
Who said, "I want to eat you now!"
The cookie man just laughed and fled.
Here is what the cookie said:

CHORUS

A farmer saw the man go by.
He chased him low, he chased him high.
The cookie man just shook his head.
Here is what the cookie said:

CHORUS

He finally reached a river wide.
A fox asked, "Would you like a ride?"
The cookie sat on the fox's head.
Here is what the sly fox said:

"You can't run! That's my plan!
I'm going to eat you, gingerbread man!
You can't run! That's my plan!"
And he ate the gingerbread man!

TEACHER'S PAGE

ABOUT THE STORY

"The Gingerbread Man" (also known as "The Gingerbread Boy") is an old English folktale. It was originally known by the title "Johnny Cake." (Johnny cake is corn bread baked on a griddle.) The story can be viewed as a cautionary tale: Individuals who boast about their abilities may someday be caught with their guard down.

SUGGESTIONS FOR SHARING

Offer each child a piece of drawing paper that has been folded down and over to create fourths. Also provide each student with an empty milk carton that already has the top half cut off. Instruct students to use their four paper segments to draw one picture each of the gingerbread man, the cow, the farmer and the fox. Next, have each student invert his or her milk carton, cut apart the paper segments and glue or staple them to the four sides of their cartons. Then, as the poem is read or recited, students should slip one hand inside their cartons and use their other hand to turn the carton so the correct character faces forward when it appears in the poem.

EXTENSION ACTIVITY (VOCABULARY/SCIENCE)

Make gingerbread cookies from scratch, or just provide a sample of store-bought cookies so students have a chance to sample gingerbread. Either way bring in an assortment of pungent spices used to make gingerbread such as ginger, allspice, and cloves. Pass these around and allow children to rely on their senses of smell and taste in order to name each spice. Also, place some cooking tools used to make gingerbread into a shopping bag. These might include a rolling pin, a spatula, a cookie tin, a bowl, a whisk, measuring spoons and measuring cups. Before taking each tool out of the bag, describe it to the class and have them guess the tool's name. Invite students to take turns describing the tools for their classmates to guess.

LITERATURE LINKS

The Gingerbread Doll by Susan Tews, illustrated by Megan Lloyd. New York: Clarion Books, 1993.

The Gingerbread Man retold by Pam Adams. New York: Child's Play, 1990.

The Gingerbread Man retold by Eric Kimmel, illustrated by Megan Lloyd. New York: Holiday House, 1993.

The Three Billy Goats Gruff

Along a hill, across a bridge
Grew lots of tasty grass.
But under the bridge there lived a troll,
A very hairy, scary troll
Who wouldn't let anyone pass!

CHORUS:
Here come the Billy Goats Gruff!
The three Billy Goats Gruff!

"I'll eat you up!" the troll cried out
To the first goat on the bridge.
"I'm small for you," Little Billy said.
"Wait for my bigger brother instead."
So the first goat crossed the bridge.
Little Billy crossed the bridge!

CHORUS

"I'll eat you up!" the troll cried out
To the second goat on the bridge.
"I'm small for you," Middle Billy said.
"Wait for my bigger brother instead."
So the second goat crossed the bridge.
Middle Billy crossed the bridge!

CHORUS

"I'll eat you up!" the troll cried out
To the third goat on the bridge.
Big Billy laughed, "Oh, just you try!"
He butted that troll and watched him fly!
Big Billy crossed the bridge.
Now they *all* had crossed the bridge!

CHORUS

TEACHER'S PAGE

ABOUT THE STORY

"The Three Billy Goats Gruff" is based on an old Scandinavian folktale. In Scandinavian folklore, a troll is a giant or dwarf that lives underground or in a cave. As with "The Three Little Pigs" and "Goldilocks and the Three Bears," this tale involves the number three, a number that educators have found has special appeal to young children in their understanding of a story.

SUGGESTIONS FOR SHARING

Give each child a small wooden cube. As you read the poem, have the children tap the blocks together to make a gentle trip-trap sound of the billy goats crossing the bridge. The block tapping should be in time to the rhythm of the last two lines of each verse and the two lines of the chorus.

EXTENSION ACTIVITY (LANGUAGE ARTS/MATH/ART)

From felt, cut three white circles of descending size to represent Big, Little, and Baby Billy Goat Gruff. Also, cut one purple rectangle to represent the troll, a long green felt strip to represent the grass and a brown semicircle to serve as the footbridge. As you read the poem, use these pieces to represent the Three Billy Goats Gruff characters on the flannel board. Ask children to talk about how they felt about these geometric pieces as opposed to more realistic flannel board characters. Also, ask children to describe what shapes and colors they would use to depict characters and settings in the other selections in this book.

LITERATURE LINKS

The Three Billy Goats Gruff by Tim Arnold. New York: Margaret K. McElderry Books, 1993.

The Three Billy Goats Gruff by Robert Bender. New York: Holt, 1993.

The Three Billy Goats Gruff retold and illustrated by Glen Rounds. New York: Holiday House, 1993.

The Little Red Hen

(sung to "Little Brown Jug")

Little Red Hen found some wheat,
Planned to make a special treat.
She asked everyone she'd meet,
"Will you help me plant my wheat?"

CHORUS:
"No!" said Dog. "No!" said Cat.
"Little Red Hen, we won't do that!"
"No!" said Duck, with a groan.
So Little Red Hen worked all alone!

When the wheat finally grew,
Little Red Hen said, "More to do!"
She asked everyone she'd meet,
"Will you help me grind my wheat?"

CHORUS

Grinding wheat hour by hour,
Little Red Hen had made some flour!
To everyone she'd meet, she said,
"Will you help me bake my bread?"

CHORUS

After all was done and said,
Little Red Hen had hot, fresh bread.
To everyone she'd meet, she said,
"Will you help me eat my bread?"

"Yes!" said Dog, Duck, and Cat.
"Little Red Hen, we will do that!"
"No!" said Little Red Hen, now done,
"You didn't help, so you get none!"

TEACHER'S PAGE

ABOUT THE STORY

"The Little Red Hen" is an old English tale. Like many other fairy tales, it is a moralistic story that tells of the rewards of industriousness over laziness. However, unlike "The Three Little Pigs," "The Little Red Hen" is not about the virtues of work as an individual effort. Instead, it promotes the idea of group effort in order to create something positive.

SUGGESTIONS FOR SHARING

Offer children each a copy of the song. Divide the class into three sections: one section representing the Little Red Hen; one representing Dog, Duck and Cat; and one representing the narrator. Read the lines of the song together carefully; have the children in each group select one color crayon to mark the lines they should sing. Then, have children refer to their song sheets when singing the song.

EXTENSION ACTIVITY (WRITING/THINKING SKILLS)

Have the children imagine that the Little Red Hen wants to accomplish one or more of the following goals. Have them make a list of all the smaller jobs that go into achieving each one—plus help them identify the big payoff for finishing each task. Help children conclude that while each part of the job requires work, some of the work can be fun and that the end result is often worth any effort.

- ❀ making a pizza (requires shopping for ingredients, making the dough, chopping the toppings, shredding the cheese, waiting for the pizza to bake, etc.);
- ❀ cleaning her house (requires picking up her belongings, sweeping the floor, dusting the furniture, washing the dishes, etc.);
- ❀ doing the laundry (requires gathering the dirty clothes, sorting the clothes, scrubbing the stains, etc.).

LITERATURE LINKS

The Little Red Hen by Byron Barton. New York: HarperCollins, 1993.

The Little Red Hen retold by Lyn Calder, illustrated by Jeffrey Severn. New York: Golden Books, 1988.

Seven Loaves of Bread by Freida Wolff, illustrated by Katie Keller. New York: Tambourine Books, 1993.

The Fox and the Grapes

A hungry fox took a walk one day.
He saw some grapes along the way.
The fox looked high upon the vine.
"Those grapes look very plump and fine!"

CHORUS:
Jump, jump! Jump, fox, jump!
Get those grapes so fine and plump!
Jump, jump! Jump up high!
You can reach them if you try!

The fox leaped high as he could go
But couldn't reach the grapes—Oh, no!
The fox looked sadly at the bunch.
"I want those juicy grapes for lunch!"

CHORUS

Again the fox leaped off the ground
To get those grapes so plump and round.
He leaped as high as he could go
But couldn't reach the grapes—Oh, no!

CHORUS

The fox was panting in the heat.
He couldn't reach those grapes to eat.
And so he sighed, after jumping an hour,
"Forget those grapes. They're probably sour!"

This story isn't true, in fact,
But it shows the way some people act.
When they can't get their wish, they say:
"The thing is no good anyway!"

TEACHER'S PAGE

ABOUT THE STORY

"The Fox and the Grapes" is one of the most popular fables by Aesop, a Greek slave who lived about 600 B.C. Like many of Aesop's fables, "The Fox and the Grapes" uses animals to teach a moral about human behavior: People often scorn what they cannot have. The expression "sour grapes," meaning contempt for something unattainable, comes from this fable.

SUGGESTIONS FOR READING

Have children be seated in chairs to read. As children read each verse, have them clap their hands together twice (two beats) and then pat their laps twice (two beats). For the chorus, have children use their feet to keep the beat: stamping both feet together for "Jump, jump!" and alternating feet to stamp out the rest of the words.

EXTENSION ACTIVITY (LANGUAGE ARTS/MOVEMENT)

Turn the poem into a mini-movement play. Tell each of the children to pretend that he or she is the fox and to follow the movements suggested in the chant. Comment on the creatively different ways children chose to act out each one. Tell the class that when they silently act out a story, they are performing mime, a physical (body language) performance often done without words.

LITERATURE LINKS

Aesop & Company adapted by Barbara Bader, illustrated by Arthur Geisert. Boston: Houghton, Mifflin, 1991.

Aesop's Fables retold by Anne Gatti, illustrated by Safaya Salter. San Diego: Harcourt, Brace, 1992.

The Children's Aesop retold by Stephanie Calmenson, illustrated by Robert Byrd. Honesdale, PA: Caroline House, 1992.

The Lion and the Mouse

(sung to "Miss Lucy Had a Baby")

A lion once was sleeping.
A mouse ran on his paw.
The lion quickly woke up
And trapped him with his claw.

"I'll eat you!" said the lion.
"You'll make a tasty snack!"
"Don't eat me," begged the poor mouse.
"Someday I'll pay you back!"

"Ha ha!" laughed the lion.
"That's funny as can be!
You're much too small to help me.
But still, I'll set you free."

It was a few days later.
The mouse heard someone cry.
He saw it was the lion
Trapped in a net nearby!

"Oh, help me!" begged the lion.
"A hunter has me trapped!"
The mouse chewed on the net ropes
Until the ropes had snapped!

The lion had his freedom,
And learned a lesson, too:
The tiniest of creatures
Can do big things for you!

TEACHER'S PAGE

ABOUT THE STORY

"The Lion and the Mouse" is one of the most popular of Aesop's fables. Aesop is the name traditionally given by the ancient Greeks to the creator of many animal fables. However, historians are uncertain if Aesop actually existed, or if he is as much a legend as his tales. The earliest written collection of Aesop's fables appeared around 300 B.C.

SUGGESTIONS FOR SHARING

Tell children you wish for this song to be performed as a finger play. Instead of offering movements and gestures, divide the children into cooperative groups and have each group devise finger movements of their own design. (Provide copies and/or tape recordings of the song for the children to listen to as they work.) Have the groups take turns performing their movements as the rest of the class sings the song. Have children notice how their movement ideas were the same and how they differed.

EXTENSION ACTIVITY (ART/SEQUENCING SKILLS/MUSIC)

Make enough copies of the song so each child may have one. Then, have each child cut apart each of the six verses of the song. Provide children with three pieces of construction paper that have been cut in half horizontally, creating six separate pieces of paper. Have children paste one verse on each piece of paper. Then provide children with crayons, markers, scissors, glue and some textural art supplies (such as yarn, felt and nylon netting or plastic netting cut from produce bags) so that children can illustrate each verse. Staple each set of pages together in order, thus creating story books children can "read" and sing.

LITERATURE LINKS

Animals A to Z by David McPhail. New York: Scholastic, 1988.

If You Give a Mouse a Cookie by Laura Joffe Numeroff, illustrated by Felicia Bond. New York: Harper & Row, 1985.

The Lion Who Couldn't Roar by Gary Hogg, illustrated by Gary Andersen. Utah: Aro Publishing Company, 1991.

Lions by Kate Petty. New York: Gloucester Press, 1990.

The Hare and the Tortoise

Did you hear about the race between Tortoise and Hare?
Go, go, go! Go, go, go!
No one thought it would be fair,
No, no, no! No, no, no!
Hare was fast with legs so strong,
Go, go, go! Go, go, go!
Tortoise only crept along,
Slow, slow, slow! Slow, slow, slow!

Round the lake they went to race,
Go, go, go! Go, go, go!
Each one at a different pace,
Oh, oh, oh! Oh, oh, oh!
Hare was so sure he was best,
Go, go, go! Go, go, go!
He ran ahead, then stopped to rest,
Whoa, whoa, whoa! Whoa, whoa, whoa!

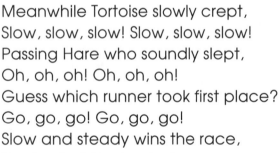

Meanwhile Tortoise slowly crept,
Slow, slow, slow! Slow, slow, slow!
Passing Hare who soundly slept,
Oh, oh, oh! Oh, oh, oh!
Guess which runner took first place?
Go, go, go! Go, go, go!
Slow and steady wins the race,
Ho, ho, ho! Ho, ho, ho!

TEACHER'S PAGE

ABOUT THE STORY

"The Hare and the Tortoise" (also know as "The Tortoise and the Hare") is another of Aesop's most popular fables. It is a cautionary tale that teaches several important lessons: don't be overconfident; don't underestimate your competition; never stop trying. The often-heard adage "Slow and steady wins the race" is an allusion to this fable.

SUGGESTIONS FOR SHARING

On each of six large index cards print the following exclamations: Go!; No!; Slow!; Oh!; Whoa!; Ho! Glue each card to a craft stick and let dry. Show the children the cards and talk about the meaning of the word on each one. Ask children to tell how all the words are alike (i.e., they are small, they rhyme). Tell children that these are all exclamations—words or phrases we utter when we feel strongly about something. Then tell children that they are going to hear a chant in which these six words appear. Read the poem through for the class. As you come to each exclamation, hold up the corresponding word card so children can read it along with you. After reading through the poem together, go back and have the children count how many times each of the exclamations appears in one line (six times). Use the cards at a second reading, this time having the children chant each exclamation in unison without your help. Finally, have the children take turns holding up the cards for their classmates to read and recite.

EXTENSION ACTIVITY (LANGUAGE ARTS/WRITING)

Ask children to brainstorm a list of some exclamations they might say when happy, sad, mad, frightened, etc. Have children interview friends and family members to add extra items to your list. Post your list in your writing corner for children to refer to. Also, consider creating a bulletin board featuring photos of the children with paper dialogue balloons printed with their favorite (and most original) exclamations.

LITERATURE LINKS

The Hare and the Tortoise by Aesop, illustrated by Arthur Friedman. Mahwah, NJ: Troll Associates, 1981.

The Hare and the Tortoise retold by Caroline Castle, illustrated by Peter Weevers. New York: Dial Books for Young Readers, 1985.

The Tortoise and the Hare: An Aesop Fable adapted and illustrated by Janet Stevens. New York: Holiday House, 1984.

The City Mouse and the Country Mouse

(sung to "The Bear Went Over the Mountain")

A mouse went out to the country,
A mouse went out to the country,
A mouse went out to the country,
To see his country friend.

They roamed the country plain,
Ate lots of nuts and grain.

But the mouse who went to the country
Said, "Life's too plain in the country."
He said to his friend from the country,
"Come see the city life!"

So the mice went into the city,
The mice went into the city,
The mice went into the city
To see the city life.

They ate sweet cake and cream.
The life there seemed a dream.

But the mouse new to the city
Soon was chased by a kitty.
He said, "This place may be pretty,
But I like my country home!"

And so he went back home,
And so he went back home.

Oh, the mouse who came from the country
Said, "Life is plain in the country.
It's plain but calm in the country,
So that is where I'll stay!"

TEACHER'S PAGE

ABOUT THE STORY

"The City Mouse and the Country Mouse" (also known as "The Town Mouse and the Country Mouse") is one of Aesop's best-known fables. The story is not an indictment of city life, but rather a tale with a simple moral: Simplicity enjoyed in peace can be preferable to sophistication accompanied by anxiety.

SUGGESTIONS FOR SHARING

After acquainting children with this song, have them suggest and collect simple props they may use for acting this song out. Then, have three students (one to play the country mouse, one to play the city mouse, and one to play the cat) take turns acting out the song while the rest of the class watches.

EXTENSION ACTIVITY (LANGUAGE ARTS/ART)

Use a vertical line to divide a bulletin board into two equal segments. Draw a ground line uniting the two sides of the display. After listing all the sights they might encounter in the country and the city, have children use paints or markers to decorate the left side of the display to represent the country and the right side to represent the city. (You may also have children use drawing paper to draw, color and cut-out illustrations of scenery and props and add these individual contributions to a basic background you've sketched on the board.) Meanwhile, trim the corners off three pieces of construction paper to create three large pear shapes (two from gray paper and one from tan paper). Have children use markers, yarn and fabric scraps to decorate these to represent the two mice and the cat. At various points on the display press small pieces of tacky display "gum." Have students move the mice and the cat on the display as you sing the song.

LITERATURE LINKS

The City Mouse and the Country Mouse by Jody Wheeler. New York: Grosset & Dunlap, 1985.

The Town Mouse and the Country Mouse retold by Helen Craig. Cambridge, MA: Candlewick Press, 1992.

Wake Up, City by Alvin Tresselt. New York: Lothrop, Lee & Shepard, 1990.

When I Was Young in the Mountains by Cynthia Rylant. New York: Dutton, 1982.

The Fox and the Crow

A crow was sitting high in a tree.
The crow was happy as she could be.
In her beak was some cheese, you see!

A fox came along and saw the cheese.
He asked the crow, "Could I have some, please?"
The crow shook her head "NO!" in the breeze.

The sly fox knew just what to do.
He said, "Oh, crow, just look at you!
Your wings are pretty, and your tail is, too!"

"Such a beautiful crow you are, my word!
You're prettier than any other bird!"
The crow liked every word she heard.

The sly fox said, "Your looks are swell.
You're very beautiful, I can tell.
I'll bet you have a nice voice as well."

"Yes, I do," thought the very proud crow.
She opened her beak to sing—but, oh!
The piece of cheese fell down below!

The sly fox grabbed the cheese and fled.
"When people praise you," the sly fox said,
"Don't let their praises go to your head!"

TEACHER'S PAGE

ABOUT THE STORY

"The Fox and the Crow" is another of Aesop's most beloved fables. As in several other stories, one of the characters is a fox, symbol of cleverness. But unlike the fox in "The Fox and the Grapes," who is unable to succeed, the fox in "The Fox and the Crow" uses his wits to triumph. The lesson of the fable is clear: Beware of flattery, for it may blind you to an ulterior motive.

SUGGESTIONS FOR READING

Discuss with children how inflection and tone can have a lot to do with the meaning behind a message. For example, demonstrate how one word such as "good-bye" can sound different when said with anger, sadness, sincerity or sarcasm. Then, after sharing the poem with the children, talk about how sincere they think the fox felt about his praises to the crow. Ask the children to demonstrate how the fox might sound if he was sincere, and then how he might sound since he is just being sly and doesn't mean his words. Then, have the children recite the poem with the fox's lines exaggerated to belie his insincerity.

EXTENSION ACTIVITY (LANGUAGE ARTS)

Have the children tell about times they were fooled as crow was fooled in the chant. How did it feel to have someone else trick them? Ask: Why are tricks usually fun to give but not always fun to receive? Is it ever OK to play tricks where you don't always tell the truth (such as magic tricks or when planning birthday surprises)? Follow up by sharing other literature selections featuring tricksters such as *Monkey, Monkey's Trick* by Patricia McKissack (Random House, 1988) or *Borreguita and the Coyote* retold by Verna Aardema (Alfred A Knopf, 1991).

LITERATURE LINKS

Crow and Fox and Other Animal Legends retold by Jan Thornhill. New York: Simon & Schuster Books for Young Readers, 1993.

Fox by Mary Ling, photographed by Jane Burton. New York: Dorling Kindersley, 1993.

Hello, Crow by Jeff Daniel Marion, illustrated by Leslie Bowman. New York: Orchard Books, 1992.

Belling the Cat

(sung to "Three Blind Mice")

Poor poor mice, poor poor mice,
Always on the run, always on the run.
They had to run from the pesky cat,
And always look where he was at.
What, oh what could they do about that?
Poor poor mice!

Then one mouse, then one mouse
Had an idea, had an idea:
"Let's tie a bell on the neck of the cat.
Then we'll always know where he is at!"
The others said, "We agree with that!"
Glad glad mice!

Now the mice, now the mice
Had to decide, had to decide:
Who is going to bell the cat?
No one was willing to do just that.
They all were afraid to go where he was at.
Poor poor mice!

From this tale, from this tale,
What can you learn, what can you learn?
It's good to have an idea, it's true,
But for the idea to work for you,
Be sure it's a thing you can really do!
Easier said than done!

TEACHER'S PAGE

ABOUT THE STORY

"Belling the Cat" is one of Aesop's most often-told fables. Like several other of his stories, this tale focuses on a struggle between the small and meek, and the large and dangerous. The expression to *bell the cat*, meaning "to take a risk for the sake of the majority," comes from this fable.

SUGGESTIONS FOR SHARING

After the children are familiar with the song, divide them into three groups and teach them how to sing in rounds. One group begins to sing the song and when they finish the first two lines, the second group begins singing. When the second group reaches the end of the second line, the third group chimes in. Each group continues singing until they reach the end of the song.

EXTENSION ACTIVITY (LANGUAGE ARTS/WRITING)

Talk about the meaning of the phrase that appears at the end of the poem: "Easier said than done." Have children brainstorm a list of things they've found to be easier said than done. Items could range from "cleaning up my room" to "being nice to a bully" to "sitting still during story time." Have children note that many of the "easier said than done" items begin as adult requests. Ask: Why would grown-ups ask kids to do things that seem so hard? Have children each illustrate and label an example of something they find easier said than done. Bind these into an "Easier Said Than Done" booklet.

LITERATURE LINKS

Belling the Cat and Other Aesop's Fables retold in verse by Tom Paxton, illustrated by Robert Rayevsky. New York: Morrow, 1990.

The Bells of Santa Lucia by Gus Cazzola, illustrated by Pierr Morgan. New York: Philomel Books, 1991.

The Kids' Cat Book by Tomie dePaola. New York: Holiday House, 1979.

The Bremen Town Musicians

There was a donkey old and slow.
Off to Bremen he decided to go.
He said, "My voice is still quite grand.
I will sing with the Bremen Town band!"

CHORUS:
Sing, sing, sing,
Sing with the Bremen Town band!

Along the way, he met an old cat,
And then an old dog—imagine that!
And then an old rooster joined them, too.
They all agreed on what they'd do:

CHORUS

But on their way, they passed a farm
With thieves inside! Oh, what alarm!
The donkey, rooster, dog, and cat
Sang out at once—imagine that!

"Hee-haw!" "Meow, meow!"
They sang as loud as they knew how!
"Arf-arf!" "Cock-a-doodle-doo!"
The thieves got scared and off they flew!

The donkey, rooster, dog, and cat
Were all so proud—imagine that!
So on the farm they agreed to stay.
Guess what they never did that day?

CHORUS

TEACHER'S PAGE

ABOUT THE STORY

Two brothers, Jakob and Wilhelm Grimm, collected hundreds of folktales from farmers and villagers around Kassel, Germany, between 1807 and 1814. They later published the tales to help preserve German folklore. "The Bremen Town Musicians" (also known as "The Musicians of Bremen") is one of the best known of Grimms' fairy tales.

SUGGESTIONS FOR SHARING

Engage your music teacher's help in having the class set this chant to music. Working line by line, have children take turns suggesting a tune for each one. The tune for the chorus should remain the same each time. Another possibility for sharing this chant is to have the children take turns sing-speaking each line. To sing-speak the chant, simply make up a tune for each line as you go along. You sing-speak one line and students take turns sing-speaking the next line. Continue alternating lines with students throughout the whole chant. The whole class can then join in on the chorus tune which should remain the same throughout.

EXTENSION ACTIVITY (LISTENING)

Discuss the different sounds produced by different animals. Try singing familiar tunes using only animal voices. For example, try singing "Three Blind Mice" using only moos, quacks or baas. Turn the activity into a "Name That Tune" listening guessing game by asking volunteers to use animal noises to sing songs while the rest of the class attempts to guess the tune.

LITERATURE LINKS

The Bremen Town Musicians as told by Eugene Evans, illustrated by Joe Boddy. Morris Plains, NJ: Unicorn Publishing House, 1990.

The Bremen Town Musicians by the Brothers Grimm, illustrated by Janet Stevens. New York: Holiday House, 1992.

The Bremen Town Musicians by Jacob and Wilhelm Grimm, illustrated by Bernadette Watts. New York: North-South Books, 1992.

Little Red Riding Hood

Little Red Riding Hood
Went traveling through the woods,
Bringing to Grandma's house
A basket of tasty goods!

A mean wolf on the way
Met Little Red that day.
He had a nasty plan
And ran off without delay.

To Grandma's he did race.
Poor Granny he did chase!
The wolf dressed in her clothes,
And in bed he took her place!

Red Riding Hood appeared,
Said, "Granny, you've such big ears!"
The wolf just smiled and said,
"The better to hear you, my dear!"

Red Riding Hood came near,
Said, "You've such big eyes, I fear!"
The wolf just smiled and said,
"The better to see you, my dear!"

Red Riding Hood came near,
Said, "You've such big teeth, I fear!"
The wolf just smiled and said,
"The better to *eat* you, my dear!"

The wolf then leaped from bed,
And chased poor Little Red.
But a hunter saved the day,
So all were safe instead!

TEACHER'S PAGE

ABOUT THE STORY

"Little Red Riding Hood," like most fairy tales, exists in several variations. The best known is the Brothers Grimm's version published in 1812, originally titled "Little Red Cap," in which the girl and her grandmother are rescued and the wolf is killed. However, more than 100 years earlier, in 1697, Charles Perrault published a cautionary version in which the wolf eats both the grandmother and Little Red Riding Hood, who had stopped to talk to the strange wolf along the way.

SUGGESTIONS FOR SHARING

Divide the class into two groups with one group playing the part of Little Red Riding Hood and the other group playing the part of the wolf. Have each group decide on a voice for their character. Then, acting as narrator, read the chant for the group. During the reading, have the children playing Red recite her dialogue in unison, and the children playing the wolf recite the wolf's dialogue the same way. The whole class can then join in chanting the last verse together.

EXTENSION ACTIVITY (SOCIAL STUDIES)

Little Red Riding Hood's troubles began when she spoke to a stranger. Remind children of the cautionary rule about never talking to strangers. Then, have children offer their ideas about what constitutes a stranger. Help children define a stranger as "someone you don't have permission to be with." Explain that, aside from not going off with people they don't know, children should always have permission from an adult in their household each time they go out to visit at another house. (Yesterday's permission to go next door does not translate into today's permission to do the same!)

LITERATURE LINKS

Little Red Riding Hood by Beni Montresor. New York: Doubleday, 1991.

Little Red Riding Hood by William Wegman with Carole Kismaric and Marvin Heiferman. New York: Hyperion, 1993.

The Little Red Riding Hood Rebus Book by Ann Morris, illustrated by Ljiljana Rylands. New York: Orchard Books, 1987.

Hansel and Gretel

(sung to "Hush Little Baby, Don't Say a Word")

There once lived a man very poor but sweet.
His children hardly had a thing to eat.
Their stepmother said, "Those kids can't stay!
We have no food! Let's send them away!"

Hansel and Gretel were forced from home,
Into the woods they had to roam.
Hansel left bread crumbs along the track,
So he and his sister could find their way back.

When they returned home, their stepmother said,
"You can't stay here! Go away instead!"
Hansel and Gretel were forced from home,
Into the woods they had to roam.

In the woods they saw, by the lake,
A beautiful house made of gingerbread cake!
Hansel and Gretel cried, "How neat!"
They broke off pieces of the roof to eat.

A very old woman in the house came out.
"Come in and eat!" she began to shout.
Hansel and Gretel were glad to be fed.
They didn't know the woman was a witch instead!

The witch planned to make both children fat
So she could eat them—imagine that!
She said to Gretel, "Get in the oven now!"
But Gretel pushed the witch inside somehow!

Hansel and Gretel found their way home.
Their father said, "From now on, you'll never roam!"
Their house was filled with joy and laughter,
And everyone lived happily ever after!

TEACHER'S PAGE

ABOUT THE STORY

"Hansel and Gretel" is one of the most popular stories from the Brothers Grimm collection. It contains several elements frequently found in fairy tales: characters lost in the woods, an evil stepmother, and a witch. As in many fairy tales, the conclusion offers poetic justice: The witch suffers the same fate that she had planned for her victims.

SUGGESTIONS FOR READING

Use hand-held triangles (or jingle bells on cords) to accompany the rhythm of the song. Play the instruments softly throughout the song—except during those parts involving the stepmother and the witch. For these parts, children should play their instruments as loudly and as jarringly as possible.

EXTENSION ACTIVITY (COOKING/ART)

Use this easy recipe to help children make graham cracker "gingerbread" cottage shapes they may really nibble on! For each cottage you need to cut a graham cracker square in half diagonally creating two triangle shapes. On a plate, arrange these triangles together to form a peaked "roof" and place the roof above another whole graham cracker. Have children use plastic knives to "paint" the whole graham cracker cottage wall with icing and the roof with peanut butter. So they can complete their cottage creations, offer children edible decorations such as: coconut, cereal bits, dried fruits, mini-marshmallows, mini-pretzels, sprinkles, and nuts.

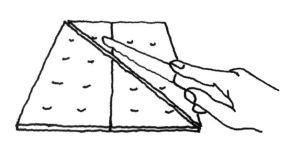

LITERATURE LINKS

Hansel and Gretel retold by James Marshall. New York: Dial Books for Young Readers, 1990.

Hansel and Gretel retold by Carol North, illustrated by Terri Super. Racine, WI: Western Publishing Company, 1990.

Hansel and Gretel: The Witch's Story by Sheila Black, illustrated by Arlene Klemushin. Secaucus, NJ: Carol Publishing Group, 1991.

The Ugly Duckling

(sung to "Baa Baa Black Sheep")

Ugly Duckling had no luck.
No one loved this different duck.
He was awkward, big and gray.
Friends and family would not play.
Ugly Duckling had no luck.
No one loved this different duck.

Ugly Duckling felt so bad.
All their teasing made him sad.
Even Mom said, "Go away!
You are awkward, big and gray."
Ugly Duckling felt so bad.
All their teasing made him sad.

Ugly Duckling went to roam,
Very far away from home.
When the winter came along,
He grew up and he grew strong.
Ugly Duckling went to roam,
Very far away from home.

Ugly Duckling met a swan.
Swan said, "Join me, please! Come on!"
"I'm an ugly duck," said he.
"You're a gorgeous swan!" said she.
Ugly Duckling's sadness was gone.
Yes, he was a gorgeous swan!

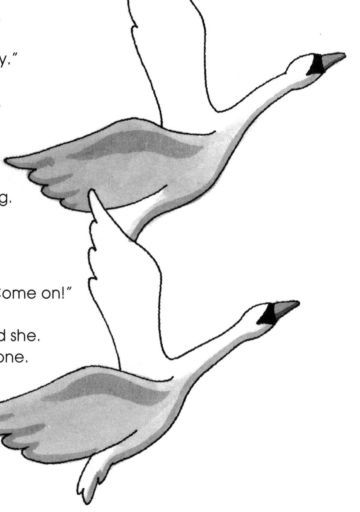

TEACHER'S PAGE

ABOUT THE STORY

"The Ugly Duckling" is a story by Hans Christian Andersen (1805–1875), Denmark's most renowned author. Coming from a poor family, Andersen saw himself as an "ugly duckling," nearly starving to death as an actor, singer and dancer before finally succeeding as a writer. Andersen never married, although he fell in love with three women, none of whom reciprocated the love. The praise he received as a writer helped Andersen ease his loneliness.

SUGGESTIONS FOR SHARING

Sing each verse of this song a bit slower than the one before it to signify Duckling's sinking feelings. Then, at the last two lines of the song, quicken the pace considerably to represent Duckling's soaring spirits.

EXTENSION ACTIVITY (VOCABULARY SKILLS/SOCIAL STUDIES)

Have children brainstorm a list of feelings including mad, sad, happy, tired, hopeful, frightened, lonely, etc. Print each of these words in the center of a separate piece of chart pad paper. Then, have children think of other feeling words that relate to the one in the center of the chart. For example, for the word "mad," children might list angry, furious, boiling, hateful, red-faced, upset, etc. Provide children with large, unruled removable sticky notes so they may illustrate times they have felt the emotions on each chart. Help children label their illustrations and stick these to the corresponding chart. Share the completed chart with the class; then post the charts in the writing corner for inspiration.

LITERATURE LINKS

Make Way for Ducklings by Robert McCloskey. New York: Puffin Books, 1991.

The Ugly Duckling by Betina Ogden. New York: Grosset & Dunlap, 1993.

The Ugly Duckling adapted by Katharine Ross, illustrated by Bernhard Oberdieck. New York: Random House, 1991.

The Princess and the Pea

Once there was a prince who tried
To find himself a perfect bride.
Yet with each princess, he couldn't decide,
For none seemed right, and he wondered:

CHORUS:
Is she a real princess indeed?
Is she a *real* princess?

Then one night, as rain did pour,
A princess came to the castle door.
"I am a real princess," she swore.
So the Queen planned a way to find out.

CHORUS

On a bed the Queen placed a pea,
Then piled 20 mattresses carefully,
Then piled 20 quilts high as can be!
And the princess slept on top!

CHORUS

In the morning the Queen asked, "Dear,
Did you sleep well on your bed in here?"
The princess sighed, "Not well, I fear!
Something was lumpy and hard!"

The Queen cried, "Son, you now can wed!
She's a real princess, as she said.
Only a real princess on top of that bed
Could feel such a tiny pea!"

She *is* a real princess indeed!
She *is* a *real* princess!

TEACHER'S PAGE

ABOUT THE STORY

"The Princess and the Pea," published in 1835, is one of Hans Christian Andersen's most popular tales. It was adapted by composer Mary Rodgers and lyricist Marshall Barer as the 1959 Broadway musical "Once Upon a Mattress," starring Carol Burnett. The Andersen fairy tale conveys a message that the author deeply believed: Real sensitivity in people is a rare quality.

SUGGESTIONS FOR SHARING

Talk to children about the concept of a "nagging doubt." Tell children that in the chant about the Princess and the Pea there exists for the Queen a nagging doubt—a tiny voice that keeps "whispering" a problematic question into her brain: "Is she really a princess indeed? Is she really a real princess?" As you recite the chant together, have children cup their hands around their mouths and use a loud whisper when reciting the chorus that features this nagging doubt.

EXTENSION ACTIVITY (MATH)

Have children use rulers (or any other measuring tool of your choice) to measure the thickness of a mattress and a quilt (or a comforter). If their quilts are too thin to measure, suggest that children fold the quilt in thirds or in fourths to get an accurate measurement. Have children bring their measurements to school so you may decide together the average thickness through which the princess felt the pea. You might try asking the children for their measurement solutions before offering one of your own (such as measuring and cutting one strip of paper to represent each child's mattress measurement and one strip to represent each child's quilt measurement and then suggesting they measure out twenty of each on a third strip of paper). (Variation: Have children each bring a washcloth to school. Place a dried pea or bean on a table and have children estimate how many washcloths (representing quilts) they can pile on the pea so they can no longer feel the bump through the cloth. After placing each one, have students test to see if they can still feel the pea through the cloth.

LITERATURE LINKS

The Princess and the Pea by Hans Christian Andersen, illustrated by Eve Tharlet. Saxonville, MA: Picture Book Studio, 1987.

The Princess and the Pea retold by Janet Riehecky, illustrated by Francesc Rovira. Elgin, IL: Child's World, 1988.

The Princess and the Pea retold and illustrated by Susie Stevenson. New York: Doubleday, 1992.

Thumbelina

(sung to "Alouette")

CHORUS:
Thumbelina, tiny Thumbelina,
Thumbelina, tiny as a thumb.

Once a magic flower seed
Bloomed into a girl—indeed!
Magic seed, girl indeed, oh!

CHORUS

On a leaf she sang each day,
Till a toad stole her away.
Magic seed, girl indeed, sang each day, stole away, oh!

CHORUS

From the toad she ran away.
With a mouse she came to stay.
Magic seed, girl indeed, sang each day, stole away,
Ran away, came to stay, oh!

CHORUS

Mouse said, "You must marry Mole,
Live inside a darkened hole."
Magic seed, girl indeed, sang each day, stole away,
Ran away, came to stay, marry Mole, darkened hole, oh!

CHORUS

On a bird she gladly fled,
Met a prince and they were wed!
Magic seed, girl indeed, sang each day, stole away,
Ran away, came to stay, marry Mole, darkened hole,
Gladly fled, they were wed, oh!

CHORUS

TEACHER'S PAGE

ABOUT THE STORY

"Thumbelina," published in 1835, is one of Hans Christian Andersen's best-known fairy tales. Like "The Ugly Duckling," it became the title of a song by Frank Loesser in the 1952 motion picture *Hans Christian Andersen*. "Thumbelina," like nearly all of Andersen's works, can be considered literature for adults as well as for children. It holds an important message: Never think less of yourself simply because you are different from others.

SUGGESTIONS FOR READING

Before singing the song, divide the class into two groups. Have the groups sing the song together except for the line in each verse that begins, "Magic seed..." At that point, the groups should take turns singing the high and low parts of the song and finish off by singing the "Oh!" in unison.

EXTENSION ACTIVITY (ART/SCIENCE)

Remind the class that Thumbelina came from a seed. Then, offer the children an assortment of seeds, plus glue and construction paper. Have them use the supplies to recreate scenes from the story of Thumbelina. They should each first decide how they might incorporate one or more seeds into the picture (a seed for Thumbelina's plant to sprout from, a seed for each of the character's eyes, a seed to place in the bird's mouth, etc.). (Variation: Research how a plant sprouts from a seed. Then, have students each glue seeds to paper and add lines illustrating how the seeds push roots down and stems up through the earth. Consider sprouting some of the seeds by placing them in soil-filed flowerpots and watering them carefully.)

LITERATURE LINKS

Thumbelina by Hans Christian Andersen, illustrated by Wayne Anderson. New York: Putnam, 1991.

Thumbelina by Hans Christian Andersen, illustrated by Alison Claire Darke. New York: Doubleday, 1990.

Thumbelina retold by Deborah Hautzig, illustrated by Kaarina Kaila. New York: Knopf, 1990.

The Nightingale

(sung to "Oh Where, Oh Where Has My Little Dog Gone?")

Oh, once in China a nightingale lived,
And every night she would sing.
With her looks so plain but her voice so sweet,
The bird was brought to the king.

CHORUS:
Oh hear, oh hear how the nightingale sings,
Oh hear her song very rare.
With her looks so plain but her voice so sweet,
Oh what, oh what can compare?

The king was pleased with the nightingale's song,
And locked the bird in his home.
So she sang by day and she sang by night,
Without the freedom to roam.

CHORUS

One day a present was brought to the king,
A gold, mechanical bird.
With its looks so fancy and voice so sweet,
This toy the king now preferred.

The real live nightingale flew away,
Back to her tree home, an oak.
And each day the toy bird would sing for the king,
Until the day that it broke!

CHORUS

The king grew sad and was nearing his death,
He missed the bird songs, you see.
So the real live nightingale came back and said,
"I'll sing if I can live free!"

CHORUS

TEACHER'S PAGE

ABOUT THE STORY

"The Nightingale" is one of Hans Christian Andersen's most often-told stories. He was inspired to write it after hearing, as a boy, how the Empire of China lay directly beneath the earth. Andersen fantasized that a Chinese prince might dig through the earth, hear him singing, and take him to his castle to become rich and famous. In a sense, the author himself is the "nightingale" in the story.

SUGGESTIONS FOR SHARING

Ask how many children know how to whistle. Then, as the rest of the children sing this song, have some of the children volunteer to whistle the chorus to simulate a bird's warbling. Or, have some of the children accompany the vocals on simple wind instruments such as recorders, whistles or harmonicas.

EXTENSION ACTIVITY (MUSIC/LANGUAGE ARTS)

Share a book and recording of Peter and the Wolf, such as *Peter and the Wolf: A Musical Fairy Tale by Sergei Prokofiev* retold by Loriot (Alfred A. Knopf, 1986). Help students understand that instruments were invented, in part, so that people could imitate the lovely sounds found in nature, including bird songs. If possible, have a birdcaller visit class to demonstrate the different sounds birds can make.

LITERATURE LINKS

The Emperor's Nightingale retold by Teddy Slater, illustrated from the Disney Archives. New York: Disney Press, 1992.

The Nightingale by Hans Christian Andersen, illustrated by Josef Palecek. New York: North South Books, 1990.

The Nightingale retold by Michael Bedard, illustrated by Regolo Ricci. New York: Clarion, 1991.

Beauty and the Beast

A merchant had a lovely daughter
Known as Beauty, sweet and kind.
When the merchant lost his fortune,
He went off for work to find.

At a palace, he met a master
Who was mean, to say the least.
"You shall die now!" cried the master,
Who looked ugly as a beast!

"Please don't harm me. I've a daughter
Whom I love," the merchant said.
Beast said, "I will spare your life
If she will stay with me instead."

When the merchant told to Beauty
All that happened, she replied,
"I will go and live there, Papa,
So that you will not have to die!"

At the palace, Beauty worried
That the Beast would not be kind.
But the Beast was sweet and gentle
And they fell in love in time.

When the Beast asked, "Can we marry?"
Beauty smiled and said, "We can."
And when Beauty said, "I love you,"
Beast became a handsome man!

TEACHER'S PAGE

ABOUT THE STORY

"Beauty and the Beast" is perhaps the best-known of the numerous fairy tales about love between beautiful and ugly creatures. The theme is so popular worldwide that probably no other fairy tale has so many variations. The first popular English version of "Beauty and the Beast," translated from a story by French author Madame LePrince de Beaumont, appeared in 1761. The 1991 Disney version of "Beauty and the Beast" changed some characters' names, including Beauty to Belle. (The word *belle* means "beautiful" in French.)

SUGGESTIONS FOR SHARING

Turn the chant into an interactive listening experience. Read the poem to the class and ask the children to listen for and react to the names of the different characters in the saga. For example, anytime the children hear the word "merchant," have them say "Yea!"; each time they hear the word "Beauty," have them sigh "AAhhh!"; and each time they hear the word "Master" or "Beast," have them say "Grrrrr!" Finally, when in the last line in the chant the words "handsome man" are spoken, have the children shout "Hooray!"

EXTENSION ACTIVITY (LANGUAGE ARTS)

In class, play the Walt Disney video version of "Beauty and the Beast." After making certain that the children understand the storyline, have children comment on the notion that someone as lovely as Beauty could fall in love with an ugly Beast. Ask them to tell what is meant by "inner beauty" and to speculate on whether it is more or less important than "outer" beauty. Use the book *People* by Peter Spiers (Doubleday & Co.,1980) to highlight the idea that beauty is in the eye of the beholder (and varies from culture to culture).

LITERATURE LINKS

Beauty and the Beast by Marie LePrince de Beaumont, illustrated by Hilary Knight. New York: Simon & Schuster, 1990.

Beauty and the Beast by Nancy Willard, illustrated by Barry Moser. San Diego: Harcourt Brace, 1992.

Disney's Beauty and the Beast adapted by A.L. Singer. New York: Disney Press, 1992.

Sinbad the Sailor

Sinbad was a sailor.
He sailed the seven seas.
He rode upon the ocean
Amid the ocean breeze!

CHORUS:
Sail on, Sinbad!
Sail the seven seas!

Sinbad found an island
With diamonds all around!
But giant birds called rocs
Soon landed on the ground!

The rocs destroyed Sinbad's boat,
So what could Sinbad do?
He tied the diamonds to his belt
And on a roc he flew!

CHORUS

Sinbad was a sailor
He sailed the seven seas.
He rode upon the ocean
Amid the ocean breeze!

CHORUS

TEACHER'S PAGE

ABOUT THE STORY

"Sinbad the Sailor" (also known as "The Seven Voyages of Sinbad") is one of about 200 stories from the *Arabian Nights*, a collection of folktales from Arabia, Egypt, India and Persia. The tales were first written in Arabic during the early 1500s. In the early 1700s, Jean Antoine Galland translated the *Arabian Nights* into French. Sir Richard Francis Burton and John Payne provided English translations in the 1880s.

SUGGESTIONS FOR SHARING

Have children act out the story as you recite it. Choose one student to be Sinbad and several others to represent the roc birds. When the story tells of Sinbad's ride on a roc bird, have Sinbad hold on to the waist of one of the rocs and have that roc lead Sinbad away. As the story is being acted out, the rest of the class can sing or recite the chorus in unison.

EXTENSION ACTIVITY (VOCABULARY/WRITING)

Print the chant on a large piece of chart pad paper. Underline all of the verbs in the chant. Then, offer children a supply of removable sticky notes and have them think of other verbs that could substitute for each of those underlined. Have children place their new verb papers on top of the original verbs. (More than one note may be used to cover the same word on the chart.) Read through the chant again and again making the necessary word substitutions as suggested on the notes. Remove each note one at a time to create new versions of the poem.

LITERATURE LINKS

Sinbad by Barbara Hayes, illustrated by Nadir Quinto. Vero Beach, FL: Rourke Enterprises, 1984.

Sinbad the Sailor retold by Patricia Daniels, illustrated by Roger Webb. Milwaukee, WI: Raintree Children's Books, 1980.

Sinbad the Sailor retold by Janet Riehecky, illustrated by Francesc Rovira. Elgin, IL: Child's World, 1988.

Pinocchio

Poor Geppetto had no son,
So he carved a wooden one,
And when all his work was done,
The puppet came alive!

CHORUS:
Pinocchio was a puppet,
A puppet made of wood!

Off to school, Pinocchio
Stopped to see a puppet show.
He turned into a mule—oh, no!
Pinocchio had been bad!

Pinocchio began to cry,
"I'll be good! At least I'll try!"
When Pinocchio told a lie
His nose grew very long!

CHORUS

Geppetto searched the stormy sea,
Wondering where his son could be.
A giant shark came suddenly
And ate Geppetto whole!

Inside he found his son, hooray!
Pinocchio helped them get away!
And for his kindness on that day,
He became a *real* boy!

No more a wooden puppet,
Pinocchio now was *real*!

TEACHER'S PAGE

ABOUT THE STORY

"The Adventures of Pinocchio" was written in 1883 by Italian author Carlo Collodi. Collodi, whose real name was Carlo Lorenzini, worked as a journalist, humorist for adults, and children's author. Through his story of Pinocchio, Collodi teaches readers the importance of being generous, honest, and industrious.

SUGGESTIONS FOR SHARING

Ask children to bring to school any Pinocchio dolls or statues they may own. When reciting the chant, display the Pinocchio objects d'art. Have children use wooden rhythm sticks or wooden blocks to tap out the rhythm of the chant.

EXTENSION ACTIVITY (ART)

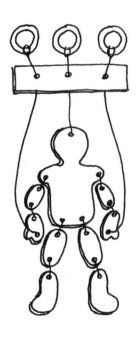

Show children a collection of real puppets—including wooden marionettes. Then, make a poster board Pinocchio marionette children may operate. First, create a Pinocchio pattern by tracing around a gingerbread boy cookie cutter (enlarging your tracing, if necessary). Cut the pattern out and cut apart at the neck, the hands, and the shoulders. Cut the legs apart at the hips and again at the knees and the ankles. Punch holes at every joint juncture in the arms. Thread a piece of string through each set of hands, elbows and shoulders. Punch three holes through a separate rectangle of poster board and thread the string up through the holes as shown. Attach ends of string to plastic shower curtain rings and manipulate Pinocchio to the beat of the chant.

LITERATURE LINKS

Pinocchio by Carlo Collodi, illustrated by Lorenzo Mattotti. New York: Lothrop, Lee & Shepard, 1993.

Pinocchio retold by Chris McEwan. New York: Doubleday, 1990.

Walt Disney's Pinocchio by Gina Ingoglia, illustrated by Gil DiCicco. New York: Disney Press, 1992.

Peter Pan

(sung to "This Old Man")

Do you know Peter Pan?
He lives off in Never Land,
Where you don't grow old as long as you are there,
You stay young without a care!

With three friends Peter knew,
Off to Never Land he flew.
There were Wendy, John, and Michael in the sky.
Peter showed them how to fly!

Down below was a crook:
Evil pirate Captain Hook!
He had captured Tiger Lily, Peter's friend,
But Peter saved her in the end.

Captain Hook was upset.
He cried, "I'll get Peter yet!"
So he sent a bomb to Peter's hiding place,
Hoping to blow up the space.

Captain Hook laughed with glee,
Stole the children, went to sea.
Then the evil pirate had an evil prank:
All the kids would walk the plank!

Peter's friend, Tinker Bell,
Said, "Poor Peter I must tell!"
And when Pete showed up, the pirate lost his smile,
And was eaten by a crocodile!

TEACHER'S PAGE

ABOUT THE STORY

The character of Peter Pan was created by Scottish author Sir James Matthew Barrie. Peter first appeared in the novel *The Little White Bird* in 1902, and part of the novel was adapted into the play *Peter Pan* two years later. Barrie also wrote a second novel called *Peter Pan and Wendy*, published in 1911.

SUGGESTIONS FOR SHARING

Take turns singing. For example, tell the class that you are going to sing the first line of each verse to them and that they are to sing the second line of each verse to you, and then you will all sing the remaining two lines of each verse together.

EXTENSION ACTIVITY (MATH)

Ask the children to tell how many times each of them has flown in an airplane. Graph the number of flying experiences they each report. Also, have them describe their flying experiences in detail. Ask: If you could each fly like the characters in the story, where would you travel to and why?

LITERATURE LINKS

Peter Pan by Sir James Matthew Barrie. New York: Penguin, 1992.

Peter Pan adapted by Cathy East Dubowski, illustrated by Jean Zallinger. New York: Random House, 1991.

Walt Disney's Peter Pan adapted by Eugene Bradley Coco, illustrated by Ron Dias. New York: Golden Books, 1989.

Anansi the Spider

(sung to "The Eensie Weensie Spider")

CHORUS:
Anansi is a spider
Who loves playing tricks.
Better beware
If you're the one he picks!
He's a clever trickster
Who stays calm and cool.
Anansi the Spider
Can make you look a fool!

Once the tricky spider
Bragged to the King:
"I take a ride on Tiger
Each evening!"
The King asked Tiger,
"Is this really true?"
Tiger said, "Of course not!
I'll prove it to you!"

Tiger found Anansi
And said, "Tell the King!
Admit you were lying
About the whole thing!"
Anansi said, "I'm sick.
Can you give me a ride?"
Anansi rode the Tiger
And cried, "I haven't lied!"

CHORUS

TEACHER'S PAGE

ABOUT THE STORY

"Anansi the Spider" is one of many tales told about the trickster spider. The stories come from the Ashanti culture of Ghana, West Africa. The Ashanti have a long-standing oral tradition that spans hundreds of years. The Anansi tales are also familiar in Caribbean culture. In American folklore, a parallel can be found in the Southern trickster stories of Br'er Fox, Br'er Rabbit, and Br'er Wolf.

SUGGESTIONS FOR SHARING

Before sharing Anansi the Spider, review with the children the lyrics and finger motions to the song "Eensie Weensie Spider." Have children describe what the hand motions that accompany this classic song signify. Then, have them work together to devise new hand motions to fit with the Anansi the Spider lyrics.

EXTENSION ACTIVITY (LANGUAGE ARTS)

Read the book *Anansi the Spider: A Tale from the Ashanti* by Gerald McDermott. Also, try sharing multicultural stories from collections that feature other fictional tricksters such as those found in *Twenty Two Splendid Tales to Tell From Around the World, Volumes One and Two* by Pleasant DeSpain (Merrill Court Press, 1990). Tell students that readers and listeners like such stories because of the surprise element involved. Ask students to tell of times they played tricks on others or about times others played tricks on them.

LITERATURE LINKS

Anansi and the Talking Melon retold by Eric Kimmel, illustrated by Janet Stevens. New York: Holiday House, 1994.

Anansi Finds a Fool by Verna Aardema, illustrated by Bryna Waldman. New York: Dial Books for Young Readers, 1992.

Anansi Goes Fishing retold by Eric Kimmel, illustrated by Janet Stevens. New York: Holiday House, 1991.

Paul Bunyan

(sung to "Oh, Susanna!")

Oh, he came from Minnesota,
So a lot of people say.
He could chop a hundred trees down
In less than half a day!

He was famous as a lumberjack,
His muscles were like rocks!
He hauled a heavy load of logs
With Babe, his big blue ox!

CHORUS:
Tall Paul Bunyan,
Chopping down those trees!
In the forest with his giant axe,
He cleared the way with ease!

Oh, Paul was quite a logger,
Full of energy and pep!
He could walk across a river
In just one giant step!

Oh, Paul could lift a mountain
Just as easy as a wink!
They say he dug the Great Lakes
Just so Babe could have a drink!

CHORUS

TEACHER'S PAGE

ABOUT THE STORY

Paul Bunyan is one of the best-known figures in American folklore and tall tales. No one is certain how legends about him originated. Some believe they came from old French folktales about giants. Others believe Bunyan was the creation of a lumber company advertising person. Still others believe he came from stories told by American lumberjacks. The first published stories about Bunyan appeared in a Detroit newspaper in 1910, based on tales the author had heard from Michigan lumberjacks.

SUGGESTIONS FOR SHARING

Have children keep beat with the song by tapping pencils (representing axes) on empty cardboard tubes or paper cups to represent logs. Have students experiment by tapping out four beats per line, or tapping on each syllable of each word of the song.

EXTENSION ACTIVITY (SCIENCE)

Explain that while in Paul Bunyan's day he was seen to be a hero because he cleared a wilderness so people could live and farm, today's heroes are those people who are aware of the importance of preserving trees or replacing the ones we cut down. Then talk with the class about the importance of trees in our lives. Books such as *The Tree: A First Discovery Book* by Gallimard Jeunesse and Pascale de Bourgoing (Scholastic, 1994) can help children understand both how trees grow and how much we rely on tree products.

LITERATURE LINKS

Paul Bunyan by Brian Gleeson, illustrated by Rick Meyerowitz. Saxonville, MA: Rabbit Ears Books, 1990.

Paul Bunyan retold by Steven Kellogg. New York: Morrow, 1984.

Paul Bunyan by Louis Sabin, illustrated by Dick Smolinski. Mahwah, NJ: Troll Associates, 1985.

Johnny Appleseed

There was a frontier pioneer
Who planted lots of seeds.

CHORUS:
Johnny, Johnny Appleseed
Planted lots of seeds!
Johnny, Johnny Appleseed
Grew a lot of trees!

He roamed across the countryside
Planting apple seeds.
"It's what the country needs!"

CHORUS

When travelers passed, Johnny asked,
"Won't you plant these seeds?
Wherever your path leads,
It's what the country needs!"

CHORUS

Across the country, orchards grew,
Thanks to Johnny's deeds!
He weeded out the weeds,
And planted lots of seeds!
It's what the country needs!

CHORUS

TEACHER'S PAGE

ABOUT THE STORY

Johnny Appleseed was the name given to John Chapman, a pioneer from Massachusetts who planted large numbers of apple trees along the American frontier in the 1800s. Historians still debate the truth of many of the legends that have sprung up about Chapman. The tales became known after an article about him appeared in *Harper's New Monthly Magazine* in 1871.

SUGGESTIONS FOR SHARING

After printing the chant on a large piece of chart pad paper (including the entire chorus each time it appears), offer children a supply of removable sticky notes so they can turn the chart into a rebus story. Have them use the notes to illustrate key words in the poem such as: Johnny Appleseed, seeds, trees, countryside, travelers, orchards, weeds. Have students count to see how many illustrations they will need to illustrate the words as they appear in each verse and chorus. Underline the words students have illustrated. Cover the underlined words with the corresponding illustrations. As you read the poem, pause slightly at each illustration allowing students to take turns removing the illustrations and revealing the words beneath. Have students store their notes (until the next reading) around the edge of the chart.

EXTENSION ACTIVITY (SOCIAL STUDIES/ LANGUAGE ARTS/SCIENCE)

Use book titles listed in the Literature Links to help students learn more about John Chapman, otherwise known as Johnny Appleseed. Follow up with an autumn apple tasting party in which students identify and sample different apple varieties including Golden Delicious, Granny Smith, Jonathan, McIntosh, Newton Pippin, Red Delicious, Rome Beauty, Stayman, Winesap, and York Imperial.

LITERATURE LINKS

Johnny Appleseed by Jan Gleiter and Kathleen Thompson, illustrated by Harry Quinn. Milwaukee: Raintree, 1987.

Johnny Appleseed by Steven Kellogg. New York: Morrow Junior Books, 1988.

Johnny Appleseed by Louis Sabin, illustrated by Dick Smolinski. Mahwah, NJ: Troll Associates, 1985.

Pecos Bill

(sung to "Jack and Jill")

Pecos Bill had super skill.
He rode a horse named Lightning.
Wrestling bears and other beasts
To Bill was fun, not frightening!

Pecos Bill was on a hill.
Out leaped a mountain lion!
Bill just rode upon its back
Until that cat was cryin'!

Pecos Bill did not get ill
When rattlesnakes would see him.
He would squeeze the snakes so hard
That they would quickly flee him!

Pecos Bill once got a thrill
Atop a cyclone spinning!
Bill refused to be thrown off
And rode it widely grinning!

Pecos Bill had super skills,
And no one could excel them.
Though these tales of him aren't true,
It sure is fun to tell them!

TEACHER'S PAGE

ABOUT THE STORY

Pecos Bill is a cowboy hero in American folklore. According to legend, he invented roping, cattle-branding, and other cowboy skills. He also invented the six-shooter gun and taught broncos how to buck. Tall tales about Pecos Bill developed from a magazine article written in 1923 by an American journalist named Edward O'Reilly. O'Reilly fashioned Bill after Paul Bunyan and other legendary frontier heroes.

SUGGESTIONS FOR SHARING

Have students sit cross legged on the floor in a straight line or in a circle. Have each student place his or her arms on the shoulder of the student to the left and to the right (or just have students sit shoulder-to-shoulder). As you sing the song, have students sway from side to side to keep the beat.

EXTENSION ACTIVITY (LANGUAGE ARTS/WRITING)

Help children define a tall tale as a story that has been exaggerated. Tall tales about Pecos Bill exaggerated his strength against enemies, elements and illness. Ask children to tell of times they may have "stretched the truth" a bit. Also, have them offer reasons why they felt the need to exaggerate (e.g., to save face, to avoid negative consequences, etc.). Finally, offer each child a piece of craft paper that has been cut into long strips. Have them hold the papers vertically and write and illustrate about the times they told their own tall tales. Bind these together at the top into a tall shape book titled "Our Class Tells Tall Tales."

LITERATURE LINKS

Pecos Bill by Steven Kellogg. New York, William Morrow, 1986.

Pecos Bill. Greenwich, CT: Twin Books/Mallard Press, 1990.

Pecos Bill retold by Patrick McGrath, illustrated by T. Lewis. New York: Kipling Press, 1988.

Rip Van Winkle

Rip Van Winkle went out one day,
Met a stranger along the way.
The stranger said, "Have a drink with me."
Rip thought, "What harm could that be?"
Rip fell asleep on the grassy lawn.
When he woke up, the stranger was gone.

Rip Van Winkle shook his head.
"I must have slept all night!" he said.
Somehow Rip felt very weird—
He'd even grown a 12-inch beard!

Rip walked home and rubbed his eyes.
The house looked old, to his surprise!
Rip thought, "Hey, what's going on?"
He called to his wife, but she was gone.

Rip walked to the village store,
One he'd never seen before!
All the folks looked out of place—
No one seemed to know Rip's face.
Rip Van Winkle told them his name.
Folks said, "A boy here is named the same!"

Rip saw the boy's mother and was glad.
He cried out, "Daughter, I'm your dad!"
"After all these years!" she cried with delight.
Rip said, "I thought it was just one night!"
Strange and funny as it all appears,
Rip had slept for 20 years!

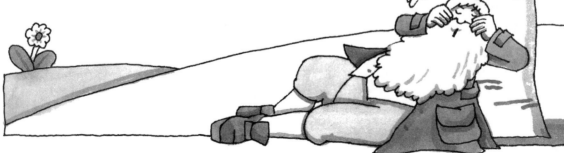

TEACHER'S PAGE

ABOUT THE STORY

"Rip Van Winkle" was written by Washington Irving. The tale first appeared in 1819 in Irving's collection *The Sketch Book of Geoffrey Crayon, Gent.* As a child in New York City, Irving listened to Dutch settlers tell legends about strange happenings along the Hudson River. Later he retold those stories, adapting them to native scenes. "Rip Van Winkle" is based on the German legend "Peter Klaus," but specific details of the setting—the Catskill Mountains during colonial times—give "Rip Van Winkle" its own color and charm.

SUGGESTIONS FOR SHARING

Record the poem on a large sheet of chart pad paper. Read aloud to the class. Then, have students study the chant verse-by-verse to discover the rhyme scheme in each one. Have children take turns using the same color crayon or marker to circle and then link the rhyming word pairs. Ask: Can you describe any rhyming patterns in this chant? Contrast this rhyme scheme with other rhyming patterns featured in the songs and chants in this collection.

EXTENSION ACTIVITY (SOCIAL STUDIES)

Have children imagine how Rip must have felt to have missed twenty years of his life. Focus them on the theme of change. Tell children that while our world is changing constantly, we don't always notice the changes because many things remain the same. (In Rip's case the changes took place over time, but he experienced them all at once.) Have children each make a list of changes large and small that they notice (in themselves, in others and in their environment) over a period of one week. Also, have children conduct interviews to find out what their neighborhoods looked like twenty years ago. Invite them to speculate about what their neighborhood might look like in twenty years.

LITERATURE LINKS

Rip Van Winkle by Washington Irving, illustrated by Arthur Rackham. New York: Dial Books, 1992.

Rip Van Winkle retold by John Howe. Boston: Little, Brown, 1988.

Rip Van Winkle adapted by Freya Littledale, illustrated by Michael Dooling. New York: Scholastic, 1991.

Casey Jones

(sung to "I've Been Working on the Railroad")

Casey Jones rode on the railroad,
As an engineer.
Casey Jones rode on the railroad,
But his tale is sad, I fear!
Casey bravely drove the mail train,
With a brave and faithful crew.
Casey bravely drove the mail train
To see the mail got through.

Casey climbed aboard the mail train
Called the Cannonball.
Casey climbed aboard the mail train
And he cried, "Let's give our all!"
Soon the train was swiftly rolling,
Swiftly rolling down the track.
Soon the train was swiftly rolling,
But it never did come back!

Casey sat up in the engine,
'Round the curve it sped.
Casey sat up in the engine,
But couldn't see the trains ahead.
"Gonna' crash!" a crewman shouted.
"Jump!" Casey yelled and pulled the brake.
He slowed the train so they could jump off,
And gave his life for their sake!

TEACHER'S PAGE

ABOUT THE STORY

"Casey Jones" is a ballad that was written in memory of John Luther Jones, better known by the nickname "Casey." On April 29, 1900, in Vaughn, Mississippi, Jones saw that his mail train was going to crash into two freight trains. He stayed on board to slow down the train, sacrificing his own life in the ensuing crash in order to save his crew.

SUGGESTIONS FOR SHARING

Choose one child to play the part of Casey Jones. Have the rest of the students line up behind each other to form a train. As you sing the first verse, the children move their arms around in circles to represent the train wheels turning. As you begin singing the second verse, the child playing Casey pretends to climb aboard the train by taking his place at the head of the line. When you sing the line, "Soon the train was swiftly rolling," have the child playing Casey begin to lead the train around the room, picking up speed as it goes. As you sing the third verse, have all the children join you in shouting "Gonna crash!" In the same verse, when Casey yells "Jump!" and pulls the brake, have the train "slow" so all the children can jump off to safety.

EXTENSION ACTIVITY (LANGUAGE ARTS)

Invite children to tell about times they have ridden on trains. Then, help the class learn more about trains using children's books such as *Freight Train* by Donald Crews (Scholastic, 1978) and *Trains* by Gail Gibbons (Scholastic, 1988).

LITERATURE LINKS

Casey Jones by Jan Gleiter and Kathleen Thompson, illustrated by Francis Balistreri. Milwaukee: Raintree, 1987.

Casey Jones by Carol Beach York, illustrated by Bert Dodson. Mahwah, NJ: Troll Associates, 1980.

The Easy-to-Read Little Engine That Could by Watty Piper, illustrated by Cristina Ong. New York: Platt & Munk, 1991.

Notes

Notes

Notes